Hello, I'm Harry the Stonemason.

Welcome to Beverley Minster. Did you know that Beverley Minster is one of the largest parish churches in England and is bigger than many cathedrals?

Come, let's explore this fantastic building. ☞

St John of Beverley

Why is there such a huge church in Beverley?

The story of Beverley Minster starts hundreds of years ago: in fact about 1,300 years. The story begins with Bishop John who for 13 years was bishop of York. When he was an old man he left York and came to live in a monastery he had founded on the site where Beverley Minster stands today. A few years later he died and his remains were buried in a chapel of that monastery.

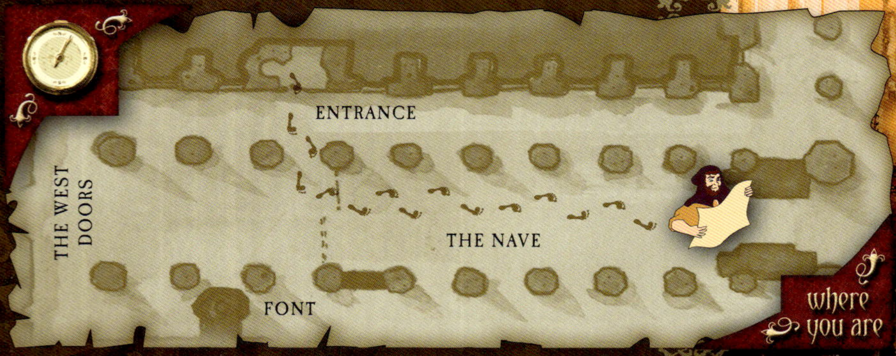

The west door from the tomb of St John of Beverley

During his lifetime John performed many miraculous healings. After his death people from all over England came to visit his tomb and ask for his prayers. Maybe they hoped to be healed of a sickness they had.

300 years after his death he was canonized and became known as St JOHN OF BEVERLEY.

Throughout the medieval period pilgrims (i.e. tourists on a religious journey) came in their THOUSANDS to visit Beverley Minster where his remains were. There are many stories of miraculous healings taking place at his tomb. One miracle recorded was about some boys who had gone blind. Oil was discovered coming from the tomb which when rubbed onto the boys' eyes helped them to recover their sight.

In this space write what the tomb tells you about St John of Beverley.

If you go to the centre of the church you will see a diamond shaped stone slab which covers the place where Sir John's tomb is.

Pilgrims put so much money in collection boxes that it became possible to build a new church to house the body of this important saint. A stone church was built to replace that small Saxon church. As more and more pilgrims came the church was built bigger and bigger and the tower higher and higher.

A new church is built

Then disaster struck. In 1188 there was a fire in Beverley which destroyed many of the houses in the town and greatly damaged the church. The fire so weakened the tower of Beverley Minster that it fell and much of the east end of the Minster was destroyed.

By this time the church was no longer a monastery but was run by a group of priests called canons. After the fall of the tower the canons decided to start again and build an even larger and more splendid church. Just imagine – they would have known that this new church would never be finished in their lifetime; in fact it took 200 years to build!

Building the new church began over 800 years ago. This is the church you are in today.

People are always asking: What is a minster? A minster is a church run by a group of clergy called canons who go out into the countryside providing services for people who have no church of their own. (A monastery is run by monks who mostly stay within the walls of the monastery and spend their life in prayer and praise to God.) Some minsters are also cathedrals – they have a bishop. York has an archbishop and Lincoln has a bishop; so these churches are cathedrals as well as minsters. Beverley has no bishop so is just a minster.

Now let's begin exploring ☞

As you go round the church follow the numbers on the plan which are on the inside of the front cover.

1. Look at the map of the church (inside the front cover)

Go to the west end of the church and stand with your back to the great wooden doors. Look directly along the whole length of the church towards the east end. What a space! Look how thick the pillars are, how high the roof, how wide the windows. Just think – 800 years ago there were no electric hoists or machines for cutting stone or even motorised cranes to lift it. All the cutting of stone, shaping, carving and lifting was done by hundreds of people, like me, called masons.

The Great West Doors

Now, turn round and look at the big wooden doors under the west window. Carved on the doors are figures of the four gospel writers who tell the story of Jesus in the Bible – from right to left; Matthew, Mark, Luke and John the Evangelist (Beverley Minster is dedicated to him).

Beneath them are their symbols – an angel, a lion, a bull and an eagle.

Between the symbols and the figures are four carvings representing the different seasons of the year.

Here is a picture of summer. Write down the symbols for spring, autumn and winter.

Spring

Autumn

Winter

2. The Font

Water poured into the bowl of the font is blessed and used by the clergy to make the sign of the cross on the forehead of anyone – baby, child or adult – who wishes to become part of the Christian family. This font was in the old church and has been in use for over 900 years. I was christened here.

Look closely at the great stone which forms the upper part of the font. This stone is very, very old – about 350 million years old! It is Frosterley marble which was brought here from quarries near the River Wear in Northumberland. Just touch the stone. Feel how cold it is. Marble is always cold.

Look closely – can you see fossils in the stone?

Can you find the dove shown on this page?

3.

Next to the south aisle door are two **lead** statues – **St John of Beverley and King Athelstan**. They are quite modern by Beverley Minster standards – only 250 years old. Over 1000 years ago, King Athelstan came to pray before the tomb of St John before he went into battle with the Scots. Having won the battle, in thanksgiving to St John, he gave rights, land and wealth to Beverley Minster.

What symbols are used to show which statue is a king and which is a bishop?

4. Every mason had his own mark which he carved on each stone he cut.

NO MARK = NO PAY!

Here are examples of masons' marks on a pillar nearest to the statue of King Athelstan. Can you find other mason's marks?

5. South Aisle Sculptures

As you walk round the church you will see many sculptures in stone. Go along the south aisle until you find these three stone heads. They are believed to be King Edward I, his son, Edward II, and his daughter-in-law, Queen Isabella. All three visited the Minster when it was being built and gave many gifts to the church.

6. Near them can you find a pedlar with a sack on his back?

7. Before you leave the **south nave aisle**, look at the windows. Above the carvings of the kings is a picture in glass of Jesus riding into Jerusalem on an ass. Just look at the colours of the glass and see how they light up when the sun shines.

When this church was built most people could not read or write. Pictures in stained glass told the stories of the Bible. Can you recognise any other stories from the Bible in the windows?

8. South Transept

From the **south choir** aisle of the nave you pass into the **south transept**. See how narrow the windows are here, while in the nave they are wider. This is because this part of the church was built before the nave.

When building a church the main problem is the weight of the roof. So at first walls were wide and windows narrow. Buttresses took some of the weight of the roof and so bigger window openings became possible.

It took 200 years to build Beverley Minster. During that time styles of architecture changed. On the left are examples of the styles of windows used. The different styles tell us, roughly, when the windows were built.

Look at the deep blue glass in the south transept window. This window is in memory of men from the East Yorkshire Regiment who fought in the First World War. The names of 7,500 men who died are written on the cenotaph in the middle chapel of the South Transept.

Early English lancet – 13th century

Decorated – 14th century

Perpendicular – late 14th century

Perpendicular – late 15th century.

There is only one window like this one. It is hidden away in the Percy Chapel on the south east corner of the church. Can you find it?

Can you see the difference between each style of window? Can you spot where they are in the church?

TIMELINE

Every day for the past 1,300 years on this site and in this church people have offered prayer & praise to GOD

Lectern – where stories from the Bible are read aloud

Year

700 800 900 1000 1100 12

721 – Bishop John dies at a monastery built on the site where Beverley Minster stands today

937 – King Athelstan visits the tomb of Bishop John

1037 – Bishop John made a saint and is known as St John of Beverley

1150 – Font of Frosterley marble placed in the Norman church

1188 – Fire in Beverley destroys much of the town and the Minster. This eventually led to the building of a new church

Edward I comes to Beverley and visits the tomb of St John

Work finishes on building of east end and transepts of the present church

Pulpit - where the teachings of Jesus are explained

1299

1300 – 1400 – 1500 – 1600 – 1700 – 1800 – 1900 – 2000

1310 Work begins on re-building the nave

1329 Edward II and Queen Isabella visit the tomb and shrine of St John

1340 Probable date of Percy canopy

1349 Many masons die in the Black Death. All building work ceases

1380 Work begins on building the west end and the twin towers

1416 New east window

1495 Probable date of Percy Chapel

1520 68 misericord seats carved

1548 Beverley Minster changes from being a church run by canons to a parish church with a vicar

1715 West doors carved showing the gospel writers

1725 Sir Michael Warton leaves £4,000 to the church

1769 Snetzler organ installed

1781 Lead carvings of St John and King Athelstan placed in church

1878 Organ screen carved

1970 Round nave altar installed by Friends of Beverley Minster

2002 New window, copper figures and seating placed in retro-quire

Altar – where Christians kneel together in prayer

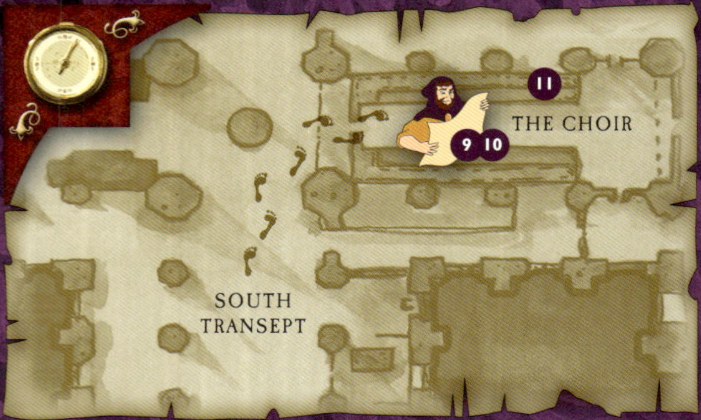

9. The Choir

Before we enter the **Choir** look at the wooden organ screen. It was carved in 1878 by a woodcarver, James Elwell, who lived in Beverley. Above it is the organ built by a German called Johann Snetzler in 1769. Note the brightly coloured organ pipes.

Once, much of the church was coloured like this.

The choir is separated from the rest of the church so that services can go on undisturbed while people wander around.

10. Choirstalls

There are 68 choir stalls in Beverley Minster – the greatest number of any church in England. This is because when these stalls were built (1520) Beverley Minster had 75 clergy and officials working for the church. Now it is run by a vicar, an associate vicar, a curate, a handful of paid staff but with a great deal of help from people who support the church and its activities on a voluntary basis.

The organ screen

11. The Misericord Seats

Services were often very long and people got tired of standing. These seats were tipped up during the service but a small ledge meant that those who needed a rest could perch but still give the impression of standing.

Misericord
= "mercy seat"
Why do you think they were called that?

Look at the carvings on the stalls. Can you see an elephant (do you think the carver had ever seen one), a monkey & a sphinx (half woman, half animal)?

Beneath the seats are cleverly carved scenes from English life. Look at these scenes. What do you think they are telling us?

Now turn towards the altar

12. Sanctuary Chair or Fridstool

On the left of the altar is the oldest chair in the Minster. It is the sort of chair on which an abbot of a monastery would sit. It was here at the time of St John of Beverley. Perhaps he liked to sit in it and rest his aching bones.

Fridstool = "chair of peace"

Sanctuary chair – or fridstool

During the medieval period anyone who had been accused of committing a crime could claim the right of sanctuary at Beverley Minster. When he or she arrived at the church an official of the Minster would sit in this stone chair and administer an oath to the sanctuary seeker. The seeker would agree to help put out fires and sing at the mass while the canons would investigate his or her case. After a month, if pronounced innocent, the seeker would be allowed to go free; if guilty he would be taken to the coast, put on a boat and ordered to live abroad for the rest of his life. The right of sanctuary existed for at least 700 years.

13. The Percy Canopy

On your left is one of the finest carved tomb canopies in England. People come from far and wide to view. Note the wonderful carving – just imagine the mason being given a block of stone and having to carve such detail onto it. I would be terrified to have such a job! One false move and I'd have to start all over again.

At the top of the arch sits God. On either side of him are two angels holding a shroud in which sits the soul of Lady Eleanor Percy asking for entry into heaven. Surrounding the arch are figures holding shields; the one in the bottom left-hand corner is a woman – I like to think that this is Lady Eleanor herself. Originally the whole canopy would have been painted in bright colours.

What colour still remains?

Percy Canopy

Lady Eleanor Percy died in 1328. She was the wife of Henry Percy, 1st Earl of Northumberland. During the 14th century the Northumberlands were one of the richest and most powerful families in the north of England. They owned a castle at Alnwick (where the Duke of Northumberland still lives today) but often stayed at their fortified house at Leconfield (two miles north of Beverley).

Now walk round to the area behind the altar. This is called the retro-choir.

14. Retro-choir

In medieval times this area would often be crowded with pilgrims who had come to get close to the gold and silver shrine of St John. The shrine was placed on the top of the reredos, the carved stone screen behind the altar. When Queen Isabella came she gave a precious jewel which was immediately fixed to St John's shrine.

15. The Warton family memorials

Beneath the reredos is a figure kneeling as though in prayer. This is Sir Michael Warton. The Wartons were a very wealthy family who lived in Beverley during the time of the Civil War. Sir Michael Warton gave £20,000 (a huge sum of money in those times) towards the cause of Charles 1.

1. The fourth Michael Warton died in 1725, leaving a large amount of money to the Minster. This money is still used today to help keep it in good repair. How much money did he leave?
2. How old was John Warton when he died?

Look at this family tree. All names highlighted are people who have memorials in this area. See if you can find them.

On the floor of the retro choir are small square brass plates. These show where the bodies of members of the Warton family were buried. The bodies have now been removed.

Warton Family Tree

✷ = buried here

- ✷ Sir Michael Warton (died 1655)
  - Michael Warton (died 1645)
    - ✷ Michael Warton (died 1688) married Susannah Poulet (died 1685) ✷
      - ✷ Michael (died 1725)
      - John (died 1656) ✷
      - Ralph (died 1708)
      - Charles (died 1714)

Sir Michael Warton (died 1655)

16. The Pilgrim Window & Figures

In 2002 a new stained glass window was placed in the retro-choir. It tells the story of a pilgrim's journey.

Note pilgrims (with hats like this) walking up the window to reach the central light which represents the love of God.

Now look how that light shines on the two copper figures on the floor who point towards the window. They are pilgrims on a journey seeking God.

Can you see a pilgrim sitting in the bottom, right-hand corner?

Come out of the retro-choir and walk down the north choir aisle.

17. The Chapter House Steps

The dark coloured pillars of the steps are Purbeck marble. This stone, much used in the first stage of building of the present minster, comes from Dorset in the south of England. No telephones, texting or computers – imagine the difficulties of ordering stone and transporting it to Beverley!

Do you think the stone would be brought overland or by sea?

These stone steps once led to the Chapter House. The Chapter House was an octagonal building (see plan) attached to the Minster in which officials of the church would meet each day to discuss matters of administration and carry out punishments on those who had disobeyed the rules of the church.

When Henry VIII quarrelled with the Pope and made himself head of the church in England all monasteries and minsters were closed down. Beverley Minster survived because as well as being a minster it was a parish church. The king gave Beverley Minster to a man called Sir Michael Stanhope who decided to pull it down and sell the building materials. The people of Beverley did not want that to happen and decided to buy it for £100. To raise the money they pulled down the Chapter House and St Martin's Church, which was attached to the southwest wall, and sold the materials for £120 – so everyone was happy!

Just imagine. If they had not got the money together there might be no Beverley Minster standing here! And I'd be out of a job!

Can you see the medallion above the doorway? It shows St John healing a boy who was deaf and unable to speak.

Walk through the doorway and into the north transept. Continue down the north aisle.

18. The North Aisle Sculptures

The sculptures along the wall are of people. Can you find the man with hands together praying? He is like the Pharisee in the Bible who thanked God for making him better than other people. But look – beneath his feet is the face of the Devil!

Four of the figures seem to be in pain. Can you guess what their illnesses might be?

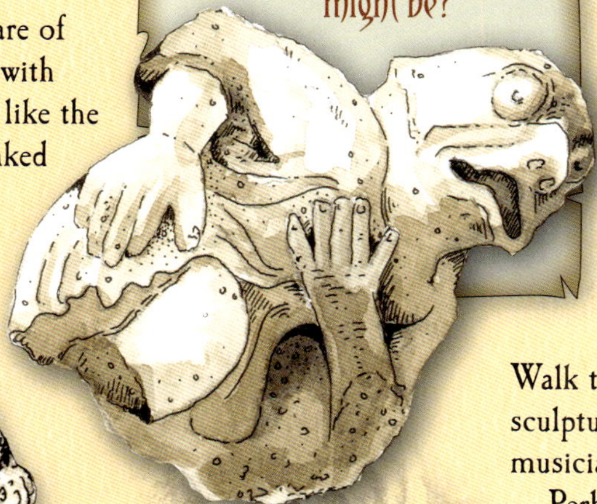

Walk towards the **Highgate Door**. Here the sculptures are mostly carvings of medieval musicians. Their bodies are twisted with dancing. Perhaps this is because they are playing the kind of music disliked by the church.

Can you find a zither player, a drummer, a violinist?

Look closely at the man playing the bagpipes. How his cheeks blow out as he puffs away! Note the detail of the buttons on his sleeve.

19. Green Men & Archers

Look at the carvings in the arches surrounding musicians and others in the north aisle.

Can you spot this green man? Green men show a face with leaves sprouting out of the mouth, nose or ears. There are over 40 green men in Beverley Minster – along the walls, at the tops of pillars, under the misericord seats. See how many you can find.

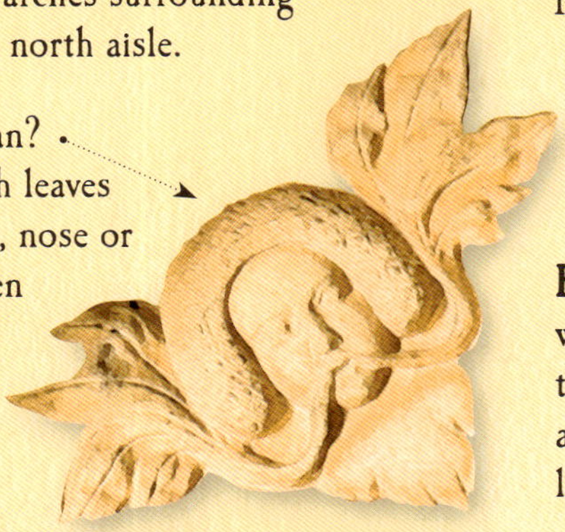

While Beverley Minster was being built the longbow and the crossbow were the most efficient weapons in battle. A skilled longbow archer could shoot up to 15 arrows a minute.

Only God is perfect. Spot the sculptor's deliberate mistake

There are four archers in the north aisle. Can you find them?

20.

One of my favourite sculptures lies hidden in the corner of the shop. It is of a man who lived in Beverley about 700 years ago. See if you can find him. I'll give you a clue: he has long hair!

I do hope that you have enjoyed our walk round Beverley Minster. There is so much to see, so much I haven't shown you. Perhaps you can come again some day.

Bye. I must get back to work. Always something to do in a building like this.

As you walk to the Highgate Door in the North Aisle, look out for me. I'll be looking for you. I have been looking out for people for nearly 700 years!